Short 'a' as in 'cat'

Find the correct word. Ring it.

| sga (gas) sag ags | ada bab bad dad | taf sat fat tta | fan san naf fna | pag qap pga gap |

Now write the word.

gas | ___ | ___ | ___ | ___

Make new words. Write them.

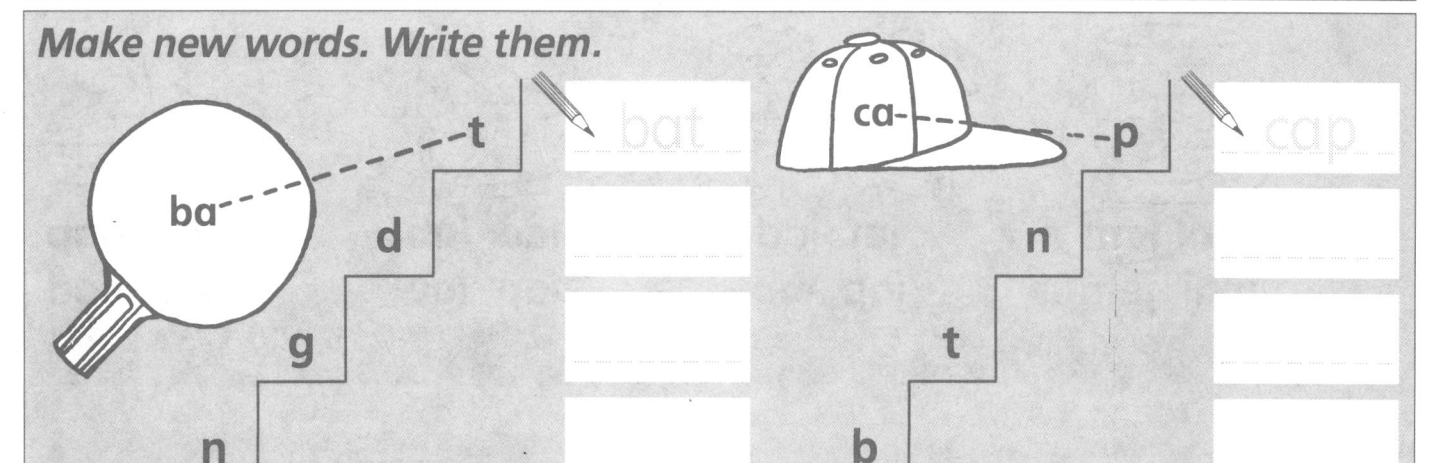

ba- -t → bat
ba- -d
ba- -g
ba- -n

ca- -p → cap
ca- -n
ca- -t
ca- -b

Complete the sentences using the words you have made or found.

We cook with gas.   I play with my _____.

Some boys wear a _____.   If I eat sweets I will be _____.

This apple is not good. It is _____.

Write the words for the pictures.

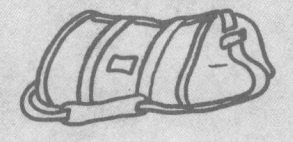

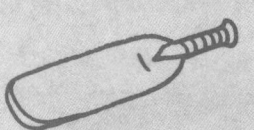

f a n | ___ | ___ | ___ | ___

Write Read Learn Spell

bat bag bad can cat cap dad gas fat fan

In your exercise book write ten sentences using these words.

Short 'a' as in 'hat'

PAGE 2

Make new words. Write them.

ha → t / d / m : hat / had / ham

ma → t / p / n / d : mat / map / man / mad

Find the correct word. Ring it.

jan (jam) maj jem

jat jad jap jab

lad lab lap lba

naq nap nab nad

Now write the word.

jam

Write the words for the pictures.

m a n

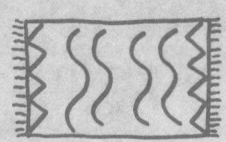

Complete the sentences using the words you have made.

We ___had___ fish for tea.   Something we wear on our heads. →

We had _____ sandwiches for tea.   The cat sat on the _____.

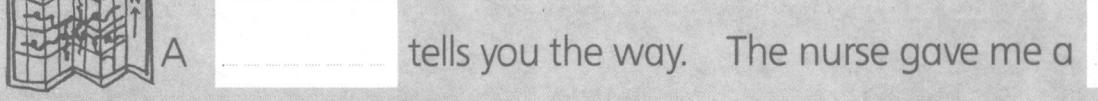

A _____ tells you the way.   The nurse gave me a _____.

Write Read Learn Spell

had ham hat jam lad man mat map nap mad

In your exercise book write ten sentences using these words.

KEY STAGE 1/2

Early Spellings
BOOK 1

boot

bib

morning

sheep

jump

NAME: _____

EARLY SPELLINGS · Book 1
by Anne Forster and Paul Martin

Early Spellings is a series of three books designed and structured to give children a firm grounding in the spelling of words used in day-to-day writing.

Contents

Book 1 (0 7217 0667 3)

	PAGE
Short 'a' as in 'cat'	1
Short 'a' as in 'hat'	2
Short 'a' as in 'tap'	3
Revision – Can you remember?	4
Little words	5
Short 'e' as in 'bed'	6
Short 'i' as in 'lid'	7
Short 'i' as in 'bin'	8
Revision – Can you remember?	9
Short 'o' as in 'dog'	10
Short 'o' as in 'rod'	11
Short 'u' as in 'mug'	12
Short 'u' as in 'cup'	13
Revision – Can you remember?	14
Revision – Can you remember?	15
Revision – Can you remember?	16
'– ll' as in 'ball'	17
'– ss' as in 'kiss'	18
'– ff – zz' as in 'cuff' and 'buzz' and Revision	19
'– ck' as in 'sack'	20
'– ng' as in 'king'	21
'– nd' as in 'pond'	22
Revision – Can you remember?	23
Pets	24
Seashore	25
Revision – Can you remember?	26
Birthdays	27
Numbers in words (1-10)	28
Revision – Can you remember?	29

Book 2 (0 7217 0668 1)

	PAGE
'oo' as in 'moon'	1
'ee' as in 'bee'	2
'oo' as in 'foot'	3
'ea' as in 'pea'	4
'ow' as in 'cow'	5
Revision – Can you remember?	6
'br' as in 'brick'	7
'cr' as in 'crab'	8
'dr' as in 'drum'	9
'fr' as in 'frog'	10
'gr' as in 'grapes'	11
'pr' as in 'present'	12
'tr' as in 'tree'	13
Revision – Can you remember?	14
'bl' as in 'blackbird'	15
'cl' as in 'clown'	16
'fl' as in 'flag'	17
'gl' as in 'glasses'	18
'pl' as in 'planet'	19
'sl' as in 'slug'	20
Revision – Can you remember?	21
'ch' as in 'cherries'	22
'sh' as in 'shell'	23
'– sh' as in 'fish'	24
'– y' as in 'jelly'	25
Doubles 'bb' and 'dd'	26
Numbers in words (11-20)	27
Colours	28
Revision – Can you remember?	29

Book 3 (0 7217 0669 x)

	PAGE
'st' as in 'star'	1
'ar' as in 'ark'	2
'aw' as in 'paw'	3
'ay' as in 'tray'	4
Words ending in ' – ey'	5
Revision – Can you remember?	6
'wh' as in 'wheel'	7
'ir' as in 'bird'	8
'ur' as in 'purse'	9
'er' as in 'flower' and 'camera'	10
Words beginning with 'th'	11
Words ending in ' – ew'	12
Revision – Can you remember?	13
'or' as in 'horn'	14
'oa' as in 'boat'	15
'ou' as in 'mouse'	16
'ow' as in 'snow'	17
'ai' as in 'snail'	18
'oi' as in 'coil'	19
'gn' and 'gu'	20
Revision – Can you remember?	21
'kn' and 'qu'	22
'ea' as in 'bread'	23
Magic 'e'	24
Magic 'e'	25
'sm' and 'sn'	26
Weather words	27
Sports Day	28
Revision – Can you remember?	29

Note to the teacher Where words appear in faint print, it is intended that pupils should write over the faint print.

©1993 Schofield & Sims Ltd.

All rights reserved. No reproduction, copy or transmission of this publication may be made without written permission.

No paragraph of this publication may be reproduced, copied or transmitted, save with written copyright permission or in accordance with the provisions of the Copyright Act 1956 (as amended).

Any person who does any unauthorised act in relation to this publication may be liable to criminal prosecution and civil claims for damages.

0 7217 0667 3

First printed 1993

Reprinted 1995, 1996 (twice), 1997 (twice), 1998 (twice), 1999

Warning
This publication is *not* part of the copyright licensing scheme run by the Copyright Licensing Agency and may not be photocopied, or mechanically copied in any other way, without written permission from the publisher.

Schofield & Sims Ltd   Huddersfield

Printed in England by Hawthornes Printers, Nottingham

Short 'a' as in 'tap'

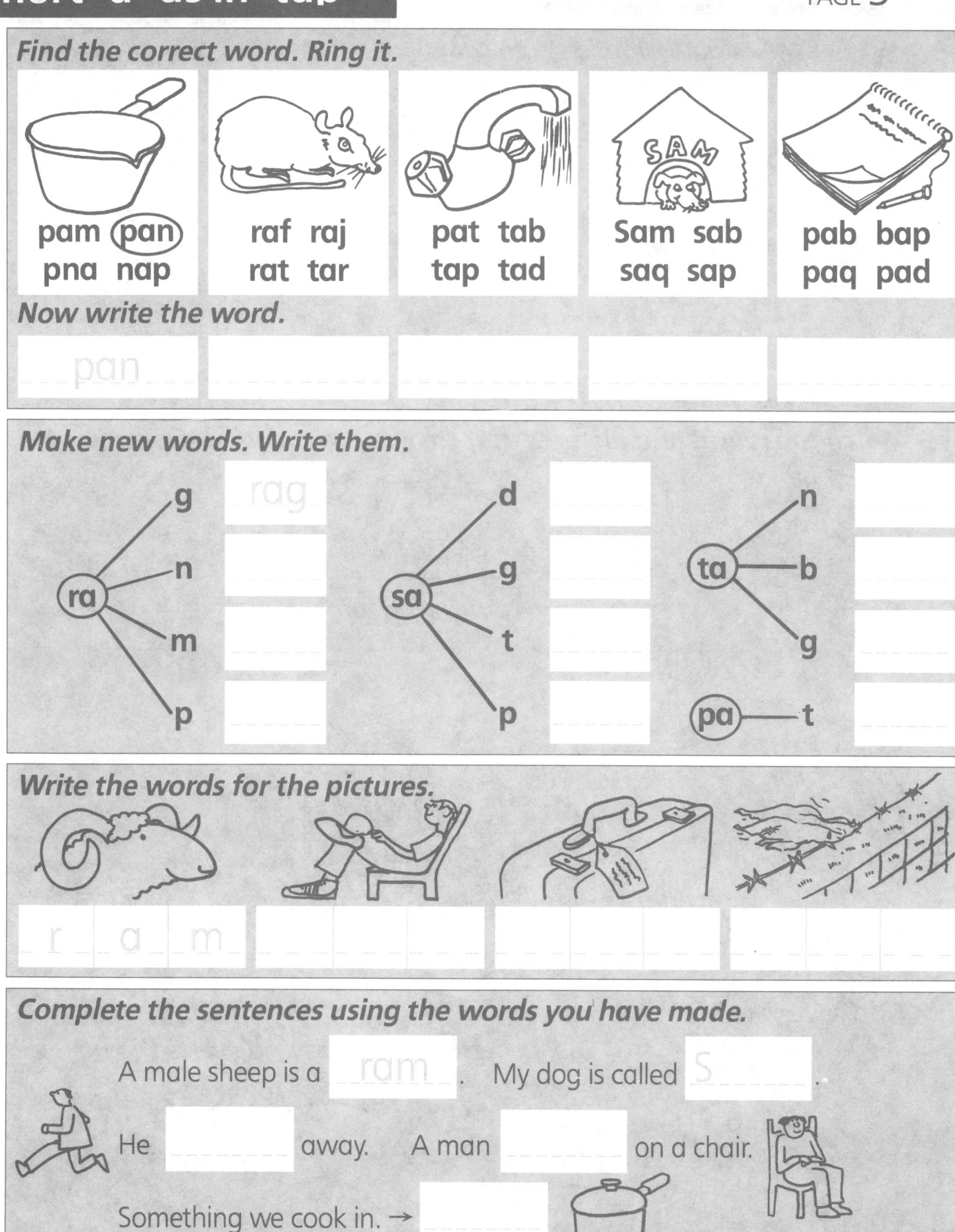

PAGE 3

Find the correct word. Ring it.

| pam (pan) pna nap | raf raj rat tar | pat tab tap tad | Sam sab saq sap | pab bap paq pad |

Now write the word.

| pan | | | | |

Make new words. Write them.

ra — g: rag
ra — n:
ra — m:
ra — p:

sa — d:
sa — g:
sa — t:
sa — p:

ta — n:
ta — b:
ta — g:
(pa) — t:

Write the words for the pictures.

r a m

Complete the sentences using the words you have made.

A male sheep is a ___ram___. My dog is called __S_____.

He _____ away. A man _____ on a chair.

Something we cook in. → _____

Write Read Learn Spell

sat sad tap pat pad pan rag rat ram ran

In your exercise book write ten sentences using these words.

Can you remember?

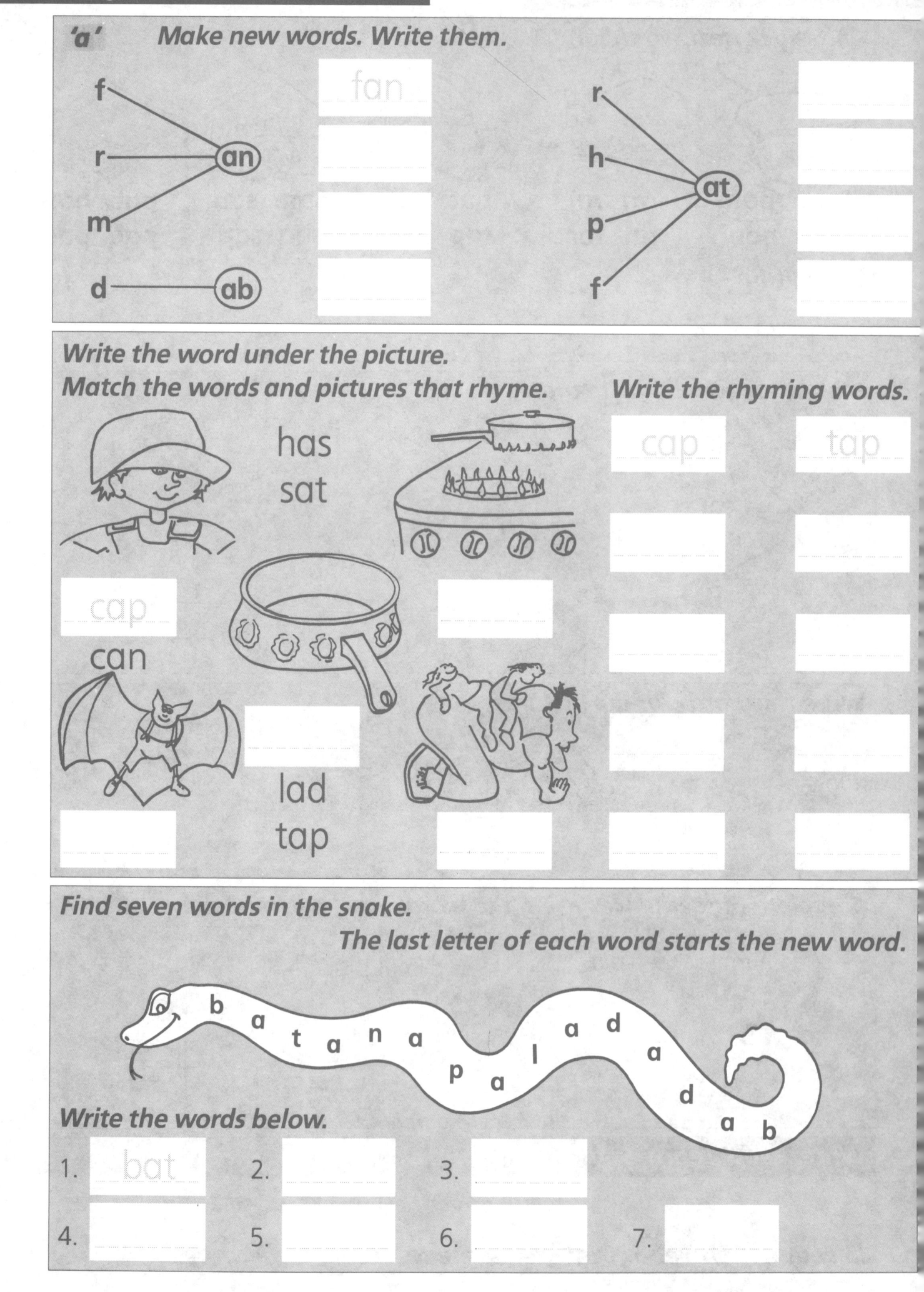

PAGE 4

'a' Make new words. Write them.

f — an   fan
r — an
m — an
d — ab

r — at
h — at
p — at
f — at

Write the word under the picture.
Match the words and pictures that rhyme.

has
sat

cap
can

lad
tap

Write the rhyming words.

cap   tap

Find seven words in the snake.
The last letter of each word starts the new word.

b a t a n a p a l a d a d a b

Write the words below.

1. bat   2.   3.
4.   5.   6.   7.

Little words

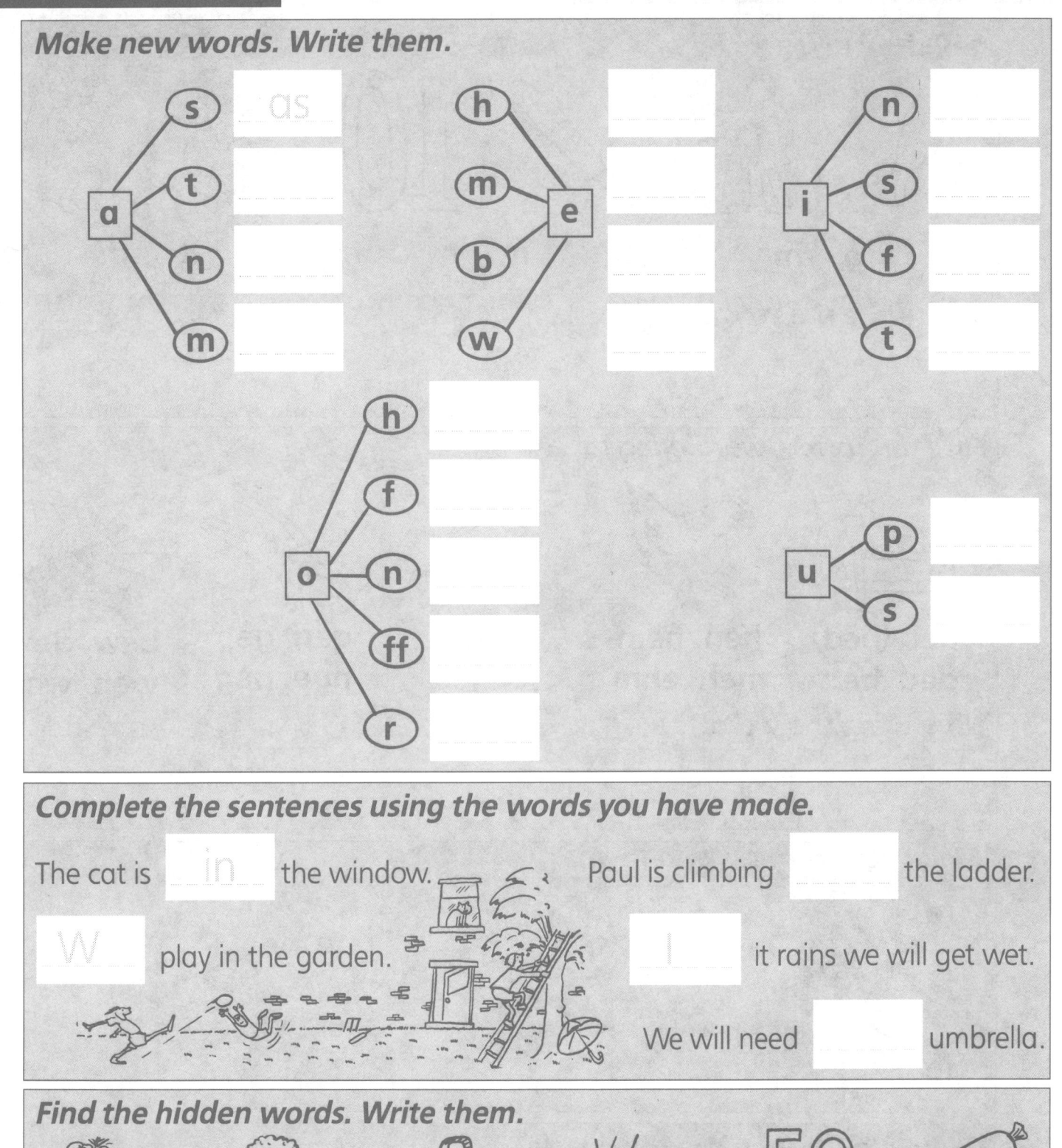

PAGE 5

Make new words. Write them.

a + s = as
a + t =
a + n =
a + m =

h + e =
m + e =
b + e =
w + e =

i + n =
i + s =
i + f =
i + t =

o + h =
o + f =
o + n =
o + ff =
o + r =

u + p =
u + s =

Complete the sentences using the words you have made.

The cat is __in__ the window.

Paul is climbing _____ the ladder.

W_____ play in the garden.

I_____ it rains we will get wet.

We will need _____ umbrella.

Find the hidden words. Write them.

plant — an
Jon —
basket —
heel —
fifty —
toffee —

Write Read Learn Spell

in is it of on up at we off he

In your exercise book write ten sentences using these words.

Short 'e' as in 'bed'

PAGE 6

Add 'e' to make a word.

| l e g | m _ n | p _ n | t _ n | p _ t | b _ g |

Now write the word.

Find the correct word. Ring it.

| deb (bed) ded beb | hen hem meh ehm | jat tej jet jek | qeg gep pge peg | bew dew web wed |

Now write the word.

bed

Make new words. Write them.

re —
le — d
fe —

we —
ge — t

le —
me — t

Complete the words in the puzzle.

I sleep in my _ e _ .

A colour. → _ e _

Not dry. → _ e _

A spider makes a _ e _ .

Write Read Learn Spell

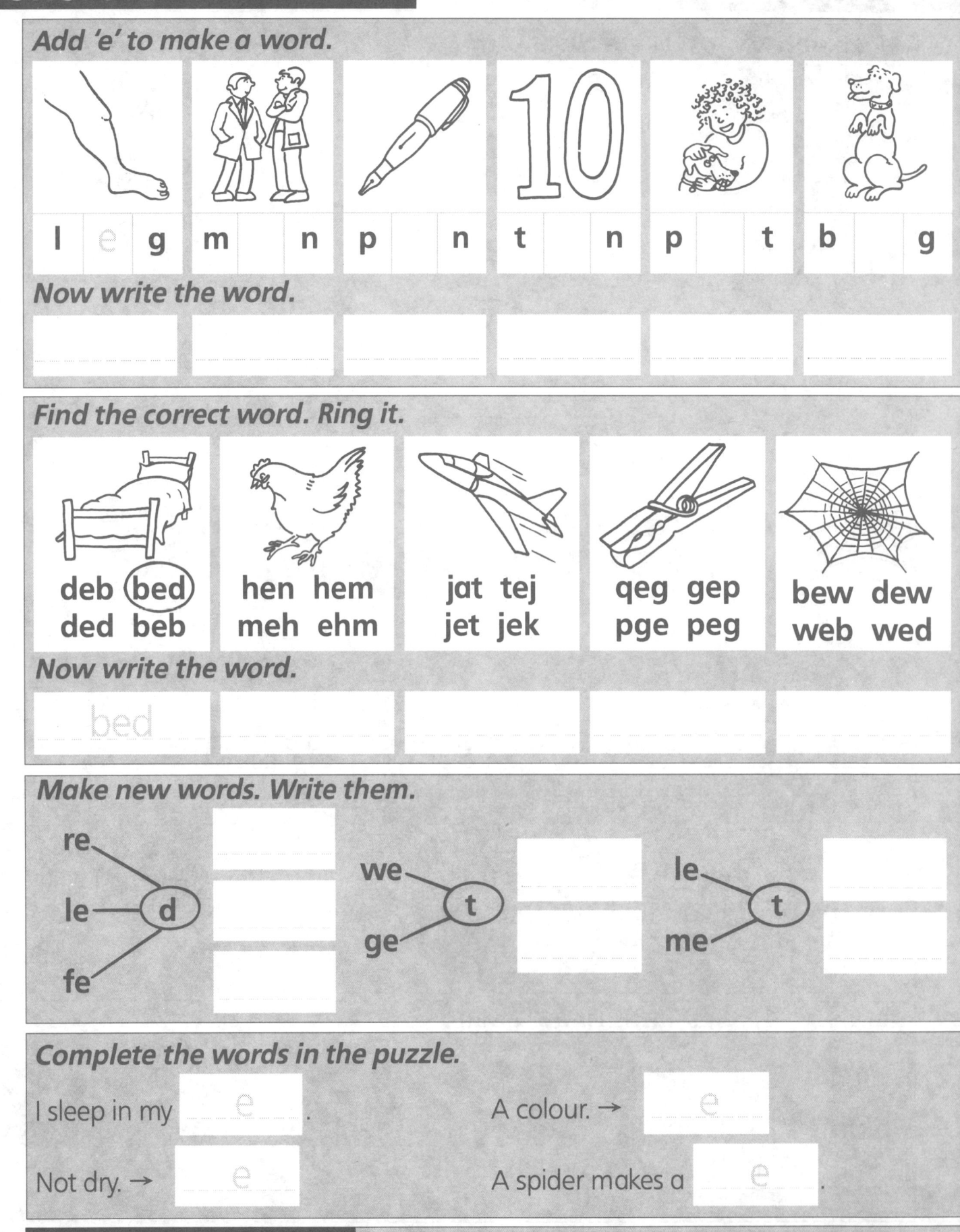

leg bed get men met pet pen ten wet let

In your exercise book write ten sentences using these words.

Short 'i' as in 'lid'

PAGE 7

Find the correct word. Ring it.

| did dip
bid (bib) | fib fid
fig fgi | kib kid
dik kip | fif fit
tif fil | fin nif
fim fiu |

Now write the word.

bib

Make new words. Write them.

hi — p, d, t, s, m

bi — d, n, t

di — p, d, m, g

li — p, t, d

Complete the sentences using the words you have made.

I _____ with my spade. I _____ the toy in the box.

The light is _____ . I saw _____ and he saw me.

The boy _____ the ball. Emma _____ her homework.

Write Read Learn Spell

bit bin did fin fit dig hid him his hit

In your exercise book write ten sentences using these words.

Short 'i' as in 'bin'

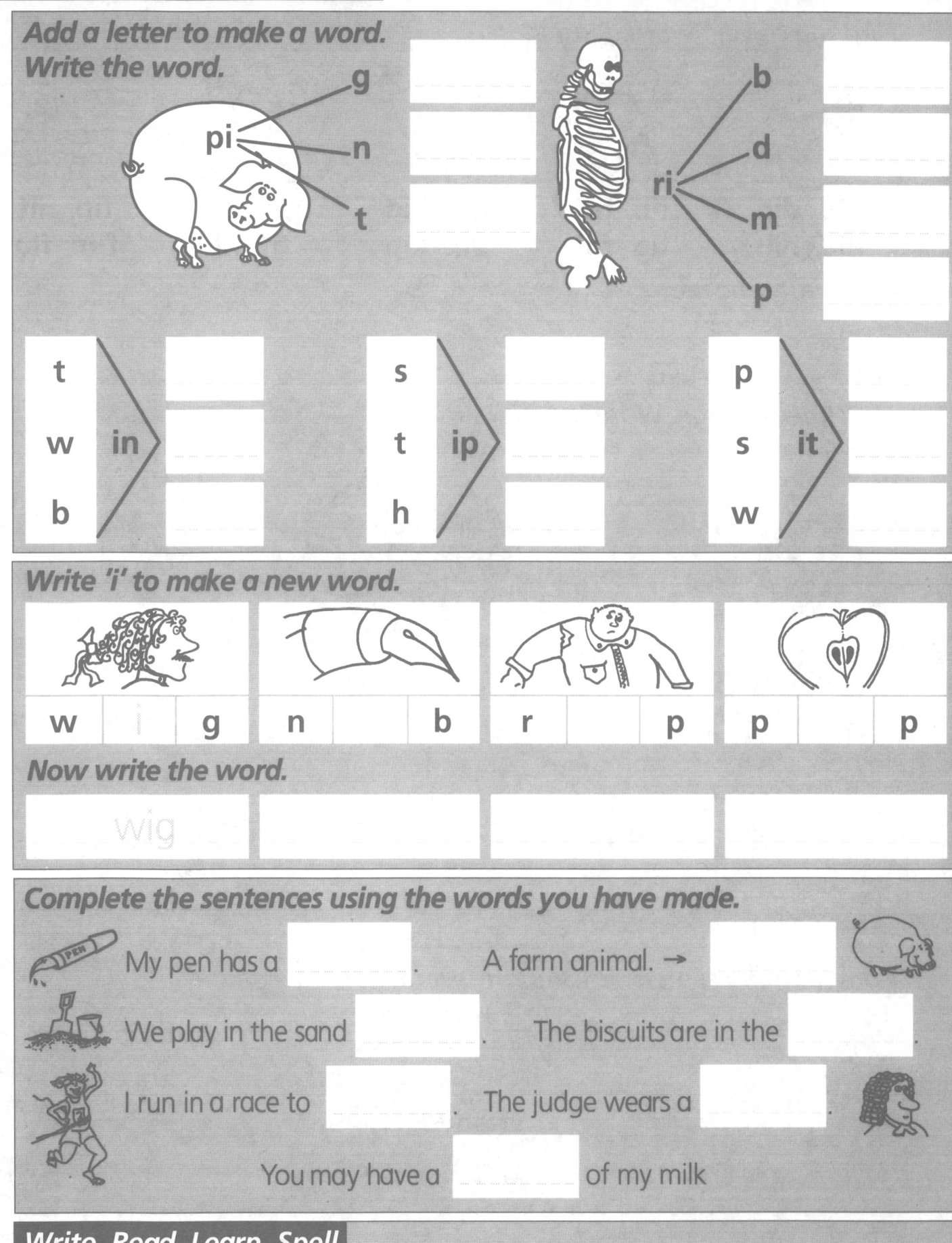

PAGE 8

Add a letter to make a word. Write the word.

pi — g, n, t

ri — b, d, m, p

t / w / b + in

s / t / h + ip

p / s / w + it

Write 'i' to make a new word.

w _ g   n _ b   r _ p   p _ p

Now write the word.

wig

Complete the sentences using the words you have made.

My pen has a _____.   A farm animal. → _____

We play in the sand _____.   The biscuits are in the _____

I run in a race to _____.   The judge wears a _____.

You may have a _____ of my milk

Write Read Learn Spell

pig pin pit rib rip pip tin tip win rid

In your exercise book write ten sentences using these words.

Can you remember?

PAGE 9

'e' and 'i' Fill in the missing letters to make a new word.

b	e	d
i		
b		

h

p

w

p

Look at the pictures. Write the words.

Write 'e' or 'i' to make a word.

1. b_n 2. b_g 3. d_d 4. l_g 5. d_p
6. g_t 7. f_g 8. r_d 9. l_p 10. w_t

In your exercise book write ten sentences using these words.

Short 'o' as in 'dog'

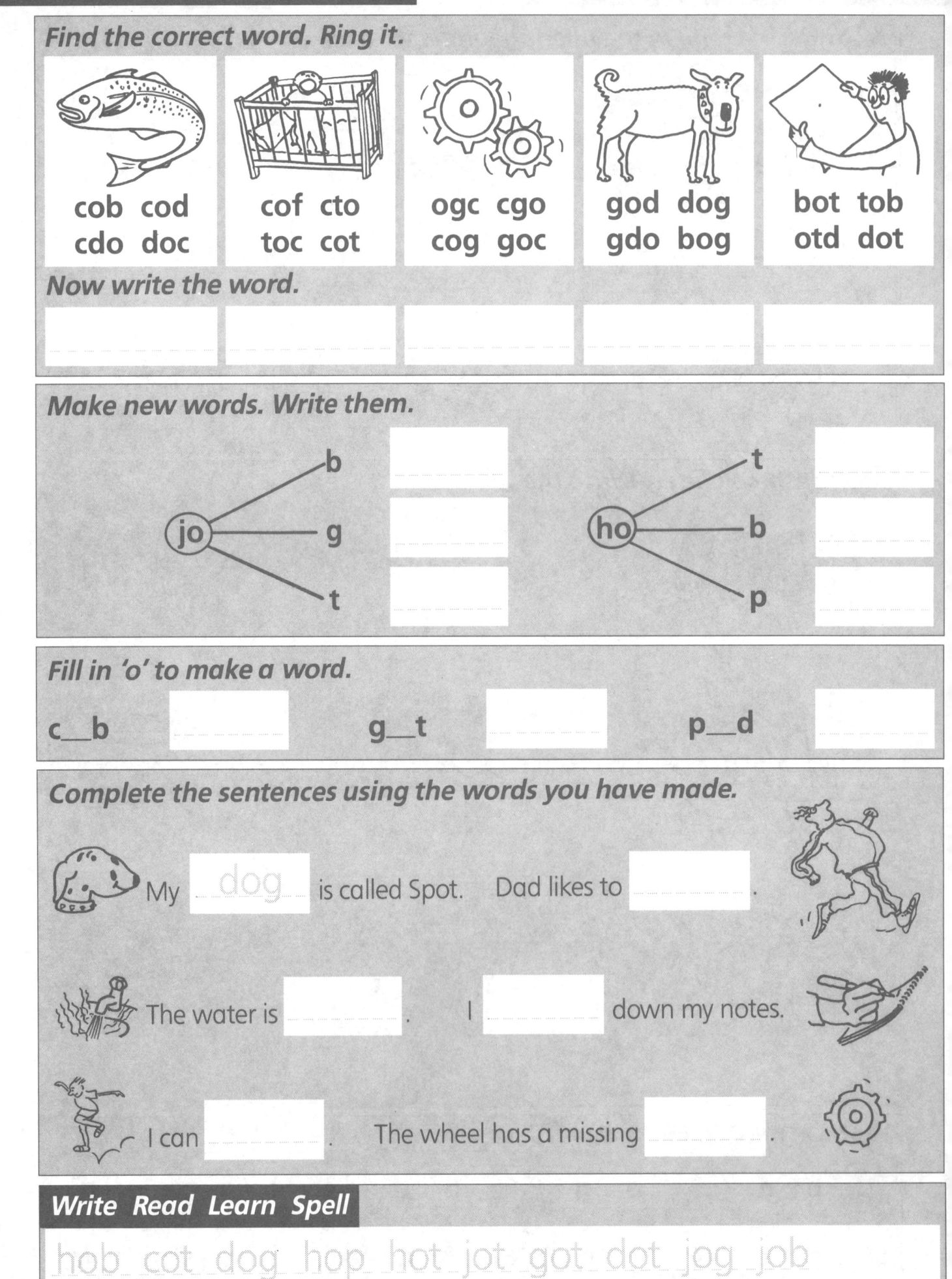

PAGE 10

Find the correct word. Ring it.

cob cod / cdo doc

cof cto / toc cot

ogc cgo / cog goc

god dog / gdo bog

bot tob / otd dot

Now write the word.

Make new words. Write them.

jo — b, g, t

ho — t, b, p

Fill in 'o' to make a word.

c__b   g__t   p__d

Complete the sentences using the words you have made.

My _dog_ is called Spot.   Dad likes to _____ .

The water is _____ .   I _____ down my notes.

I can _____ .   The wheel has a missing _____ .

Write Read Learn Spell

hob cot dog hop hot jot got dot jog job

In your exercise book write ten sentences using these words.

Short 'o' as in 'rod'

PAGE 11

Find the correct word. Ring it.

|  nop wop mpo mop |  rob bor rod rop |  tod top toq tob |  sob sop osd sap |

Now write the word.

Join 3 letters to make a word. Write the words.

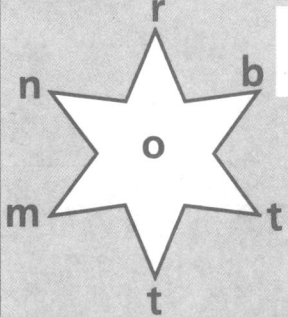

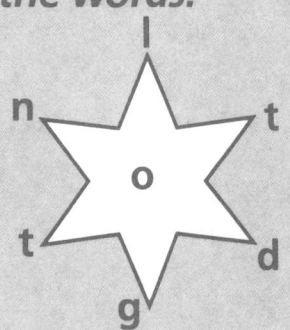

Star 1 with centre 'o' and points: r, b, t, t, m, n

Star 2 with centre 'o' and points: l, t, d, g, t, n

Complete the words in the puzzle.

Do . . . touch!

Crowd of people. → . . .

To cry. → . . .

I have a . . . of friends.

I fish with my . . . .

Part of a tree. → . . .

I can . . . my head to say yes.

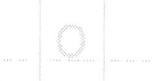

(puzzle column with o's)

Write Read Learn Spell

log lot mop nod not top sob rob rod rot

In your exercise book write ten sentences using these words.

Short 'u' as in 'mug'

PAGE 12

Write 'u' in the middle to make a word.

| j u g | m _ g | n _ t | p _ p | r _ g | s _ n |

Now write the word.

Join 3 letters to make a word. Write the words.

Star 1 letters: p, b, d, n, r, m, t (around u)

pub
___
___
___

Star 2 letters: p, b, g, m, t, r, s (around u)

___
___
___
___

Complete the words in the puzzle.

Adults can buy drinks at the . . .   _ u _

5 + 5 is a . . .   _ u _

. . . on your coat.   _ u _

I can . . . very fast.   _ u _

The cat sat on the . . .   _ u _

Rub a dub dub three men in a . . .   _ u _

Write Read Learn Spell

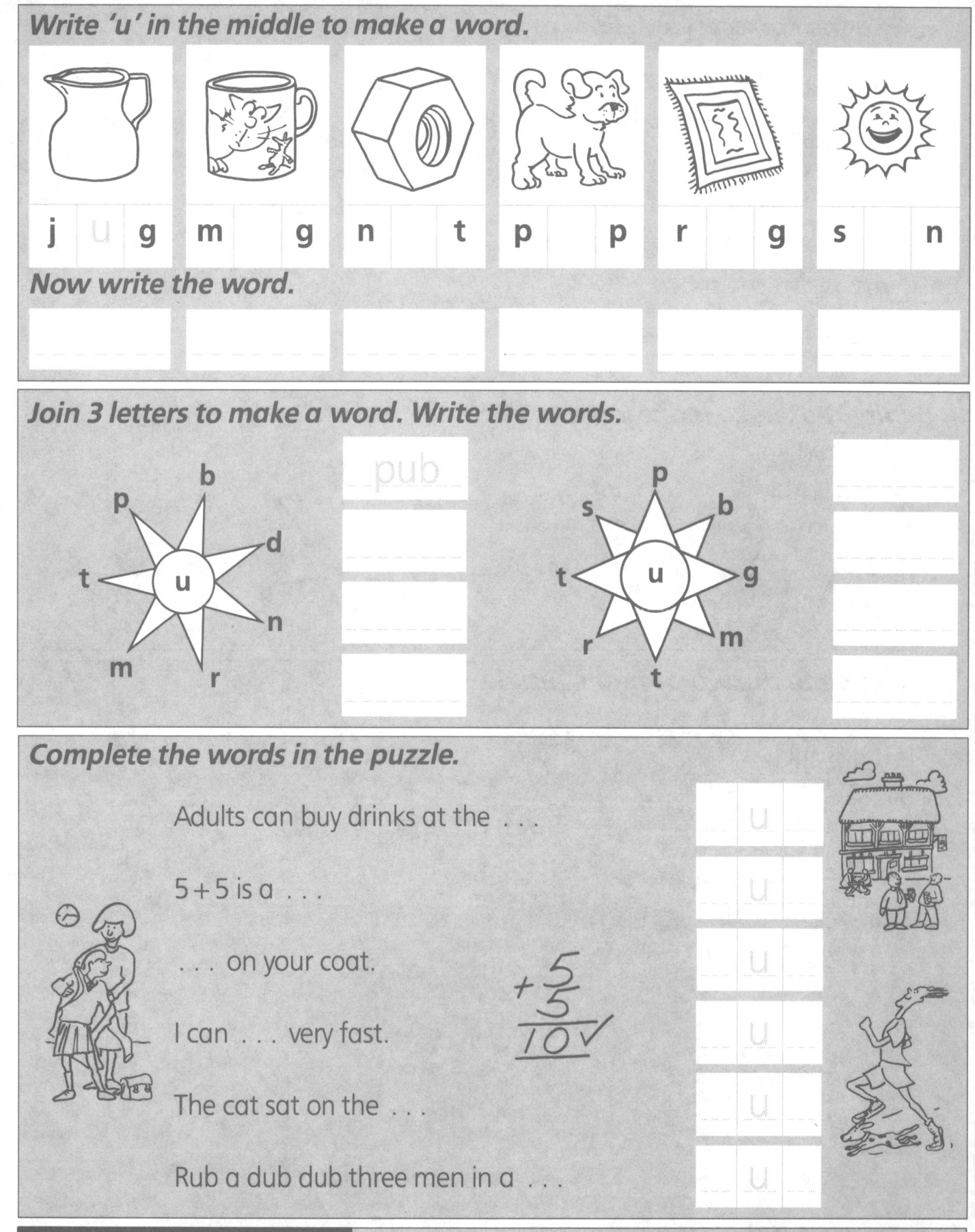

jug mug nut pub put mud pup sum sun tug

In your exercise book write ten sentences using these words.

Short 'u' as in 'cup'

PAGE 13

Make new words. Write them.

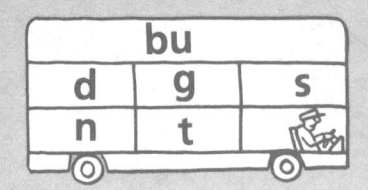

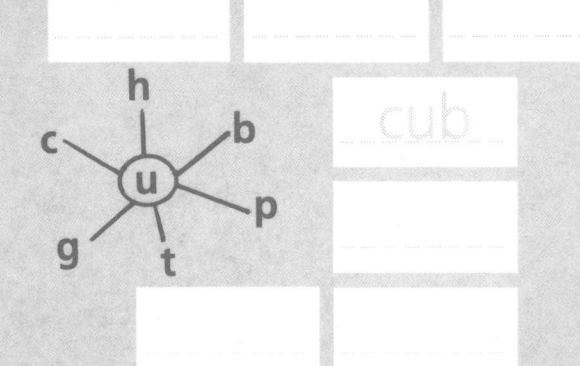

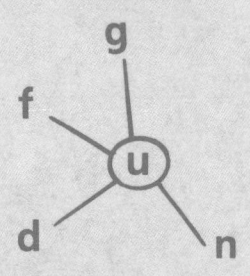

bu / d g s / n t

bud

hu / g / b t m

c h b / u / g t p

cub

g f / u / d n

Write the word under the picture.

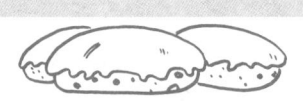

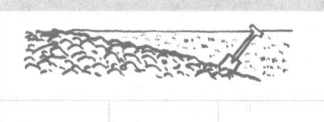

b u d

bud.

Complete the sentences using the words you have made.

We drink tea out of a cup .   The tree is in _____ .

I _____ my Mum and Dad.   A baby lion is a _____

Mum made a _____ for me to eat.

Write Read Learn Spell

bun cup bus bug bud cub but fun cut dug

In your exercise book write ten sentences using these words.

Can you remember?

PAGE 14

'o' and 'u'   Look at the pictures. Write the words.

bud

Add 'o' or 'u' to make a word. Complete the word.

| b | o | g | p | _ | t | g | _ | t | d | _ | g | h | _ | p |
| l | _ | _ | f | _ | n | _ | t | p | _ | h | _ | t | s | b |

Complete the words in the puzzle.

1. t u b   1. Three men in a . . .
2.
3.
4. wet soil
5.
6.
7.
8.
9.
10.
11. a tiny insect
12. Have you . . . a pet?
13.
14. a pea . . .

Can you remember?

PAGE 15

a e i o u   **Write twelve words in the snake.
The last letter of each word starts the next word.**

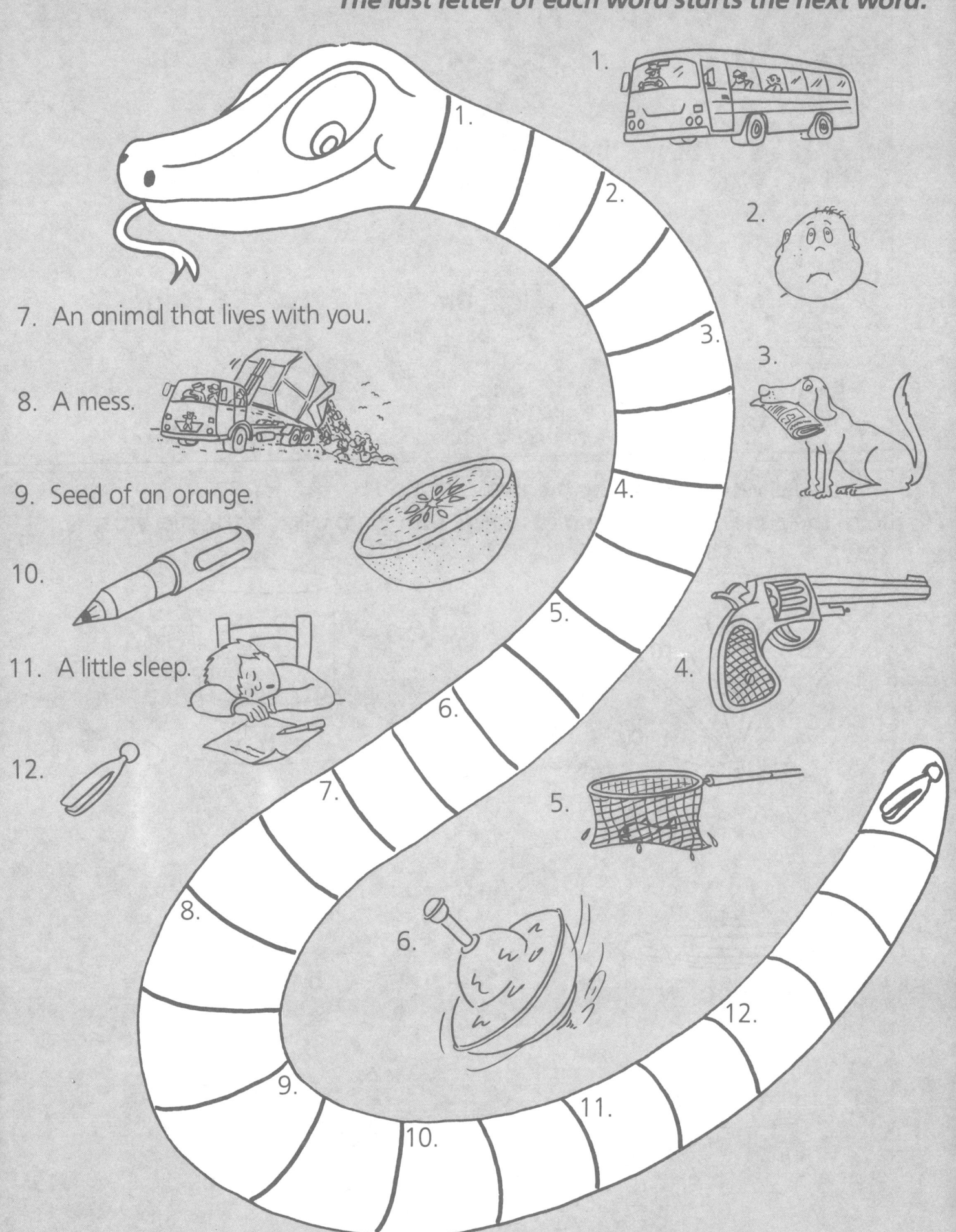

7. An animal that lives with you.

8. A mess.

9. Seed of an orange.

10.

11. A little sleep.

12.

Can you remember?

PAGE 16

a e i o u   **Match the letters to make a new word.   Write the word.**

j — at
c — am   cat
b — ap   jam
c — un

m — ot
s — op
m — un
c — at

m — um
t — od
r — en
s — ug

Write the word under the picture.
Use the other letters to make words that rhyme with the pictures.

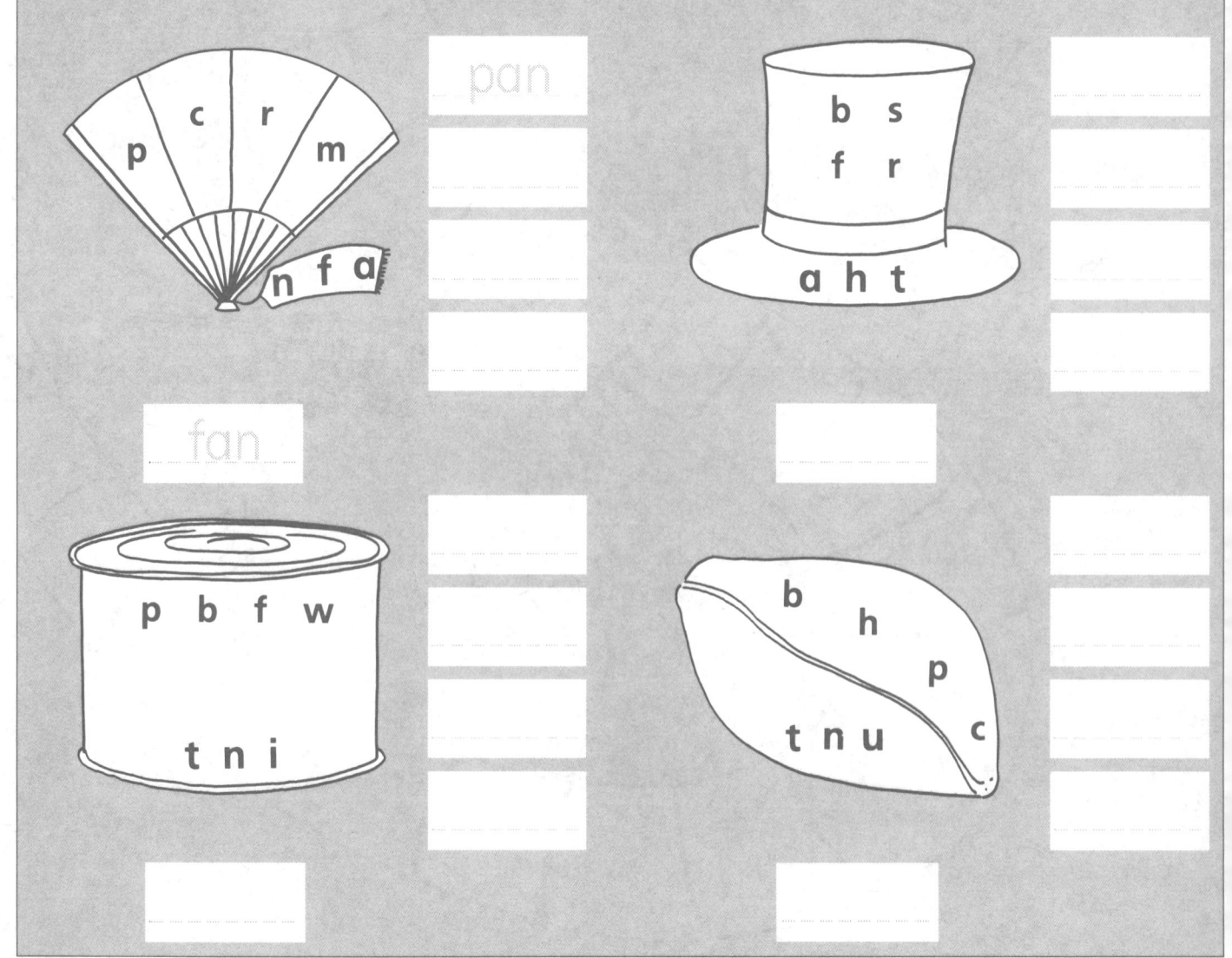

p c r m n f a   pan

fan

p b f w t n i

b s f r a h t

b h p t n u c

'–ll' as in 'ball'

PAGE 17

Make new words to rhyme with this first word.

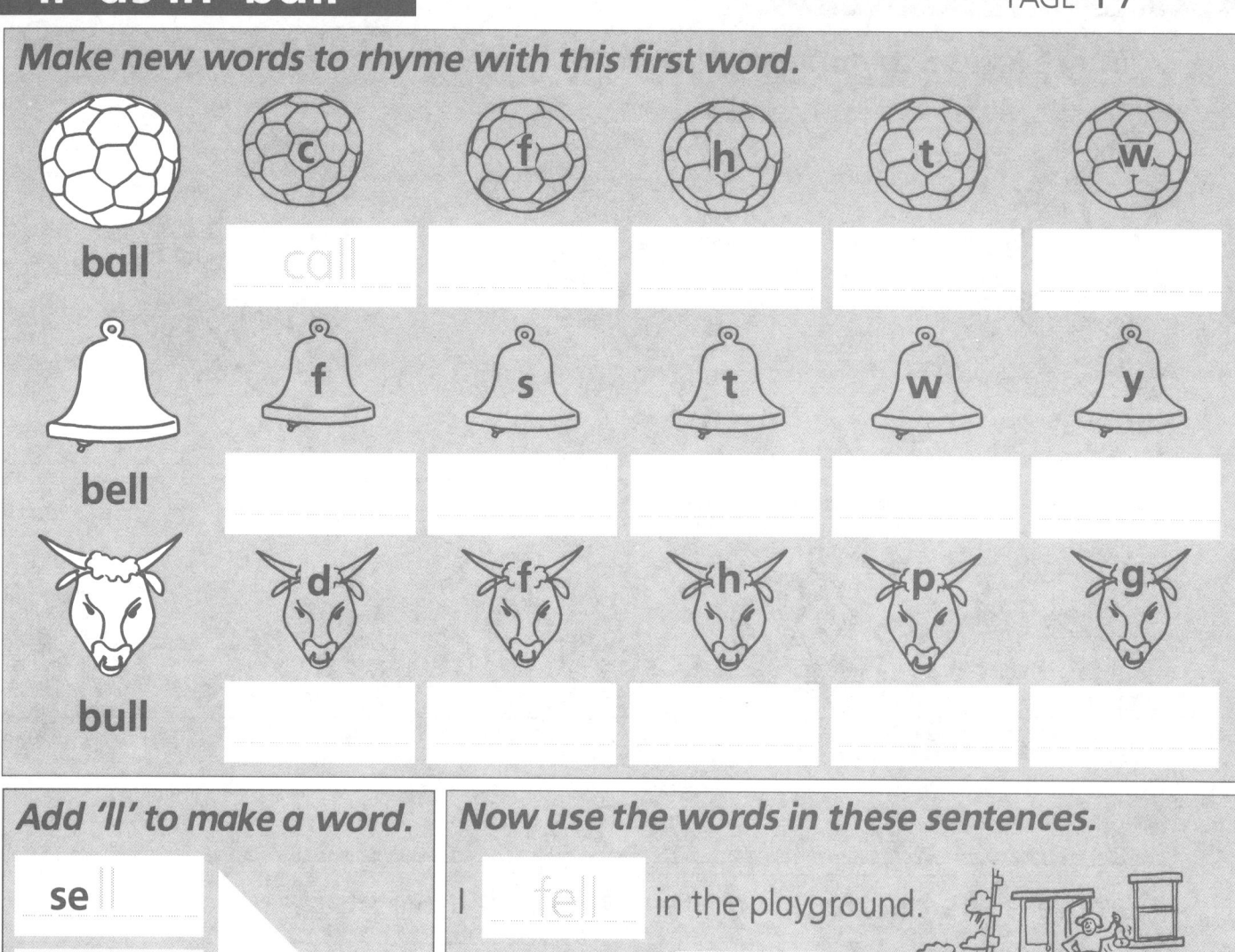

ball — call — c, f, h, t, w

bell — f, s, t, w, y

bull — d, f, h, p, g

Add 'll' to make a word.

- sell
- fe
- du
- do
- be

Now use the words in these sentences.

I fell in the playground.

I play with my _____.

I heard the _____ ring.

Florists _____ flowers.

It is a _____ day.

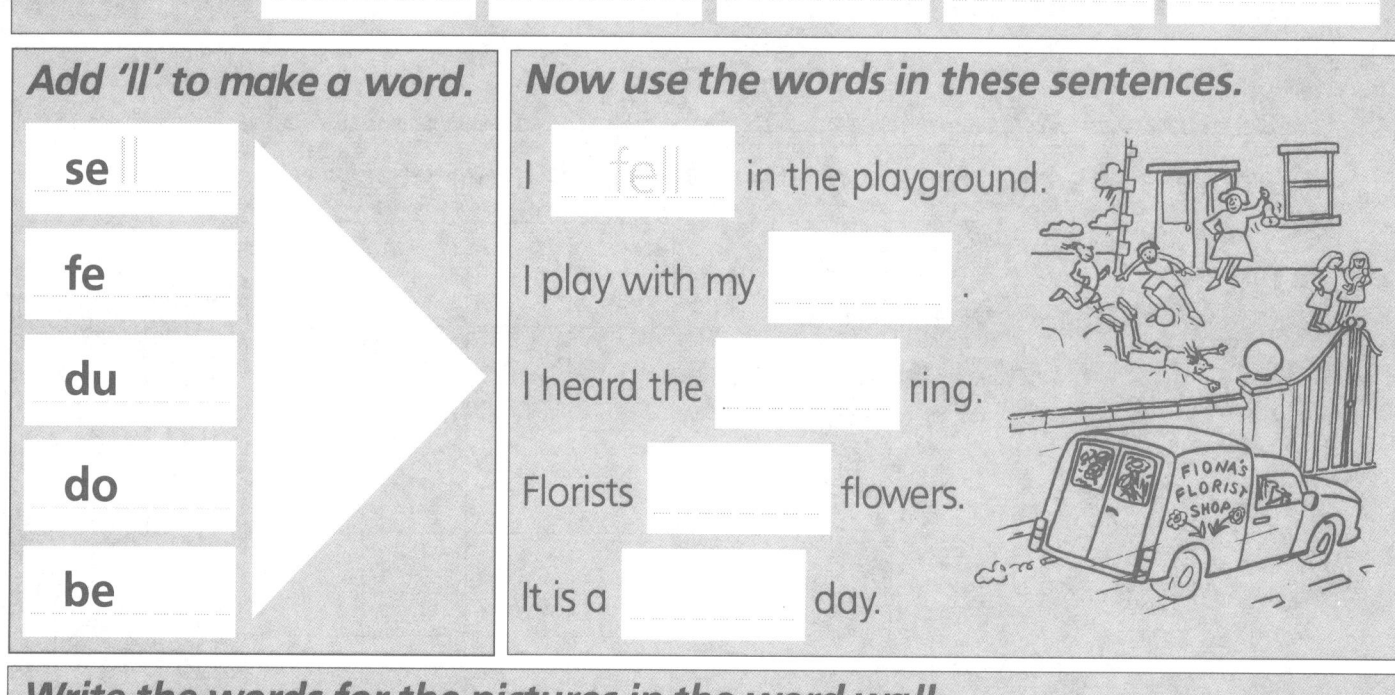

Write the words for the pictures in the word wall.

well

Write Read Learn Spell

bull bell call tell doll fell full well hall pull

In your exercise book write ten sentences using these words.

'–ss' as in 'kiss'

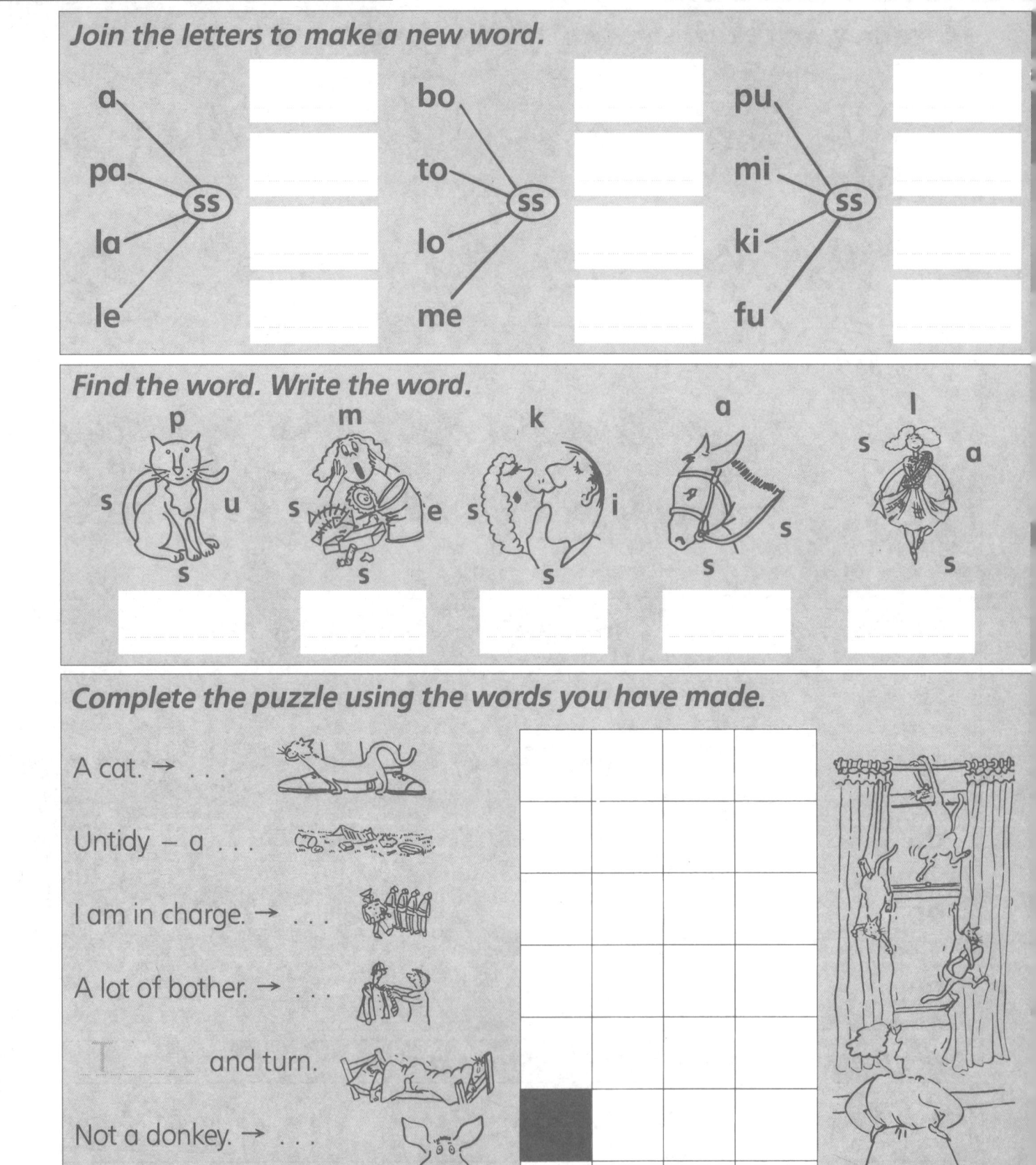

PAGE 18

Join the letters to make a new word.

a, pa, la, le → ss

bo, to, lo, me → ss

pu, mi, ki, fu → ss

Find the word. Write the word.

puss

mess

kiss

ass

lass

Complete the puzzle using the words you have made.

A cat. → ...

Untidy – a ...

I am in charge. → ...

A lot of bother. → ...

T____ and turn.

Not a donkey. → ...

I like playing ... the parcel.

Write Read Learn Spell

pass less miss kiss fuss boss toss loss puss mess

In your exercise book write ten sentences using these words.

'– ff' and '– zz' as in 'cuff' and 'buzz'   PAGE 19

Make new words. Write the words.

o — ff   cu — ff   hu — ff   pu — ff   bu — zz   fu — zz

Complete the sentences using the words you have made.

The wolf said I'll _____ and I'll _____ and I'll blow your house down.

A shirt sleeve has a _____ .   Jump _____ the wall.

The bees _____ round the flowers.

Write Read Learn Spell

off   cuff   huff   puff   buzz   fuzz

In your exercise book write six sentences using these words.

Can you remember? – ff – ll – ss   **Complete the puzzle.**

I can catch a . . . .

Don't . . . over.

The . . . rang.

A seaside bird. → . . . .

I will . . . you.

We . . . the shops on the way.

Turn . . . the light.

I saw a . . . of smoke.

. . . the hoop down the hill.

Some shops . . . food.

Children play with a . . . .

Not a cow → . . . .

b				
f				
b				
g				
m				
p				
b				
p				
r				
s				
d				
b				

'– ck' as in 'sack'

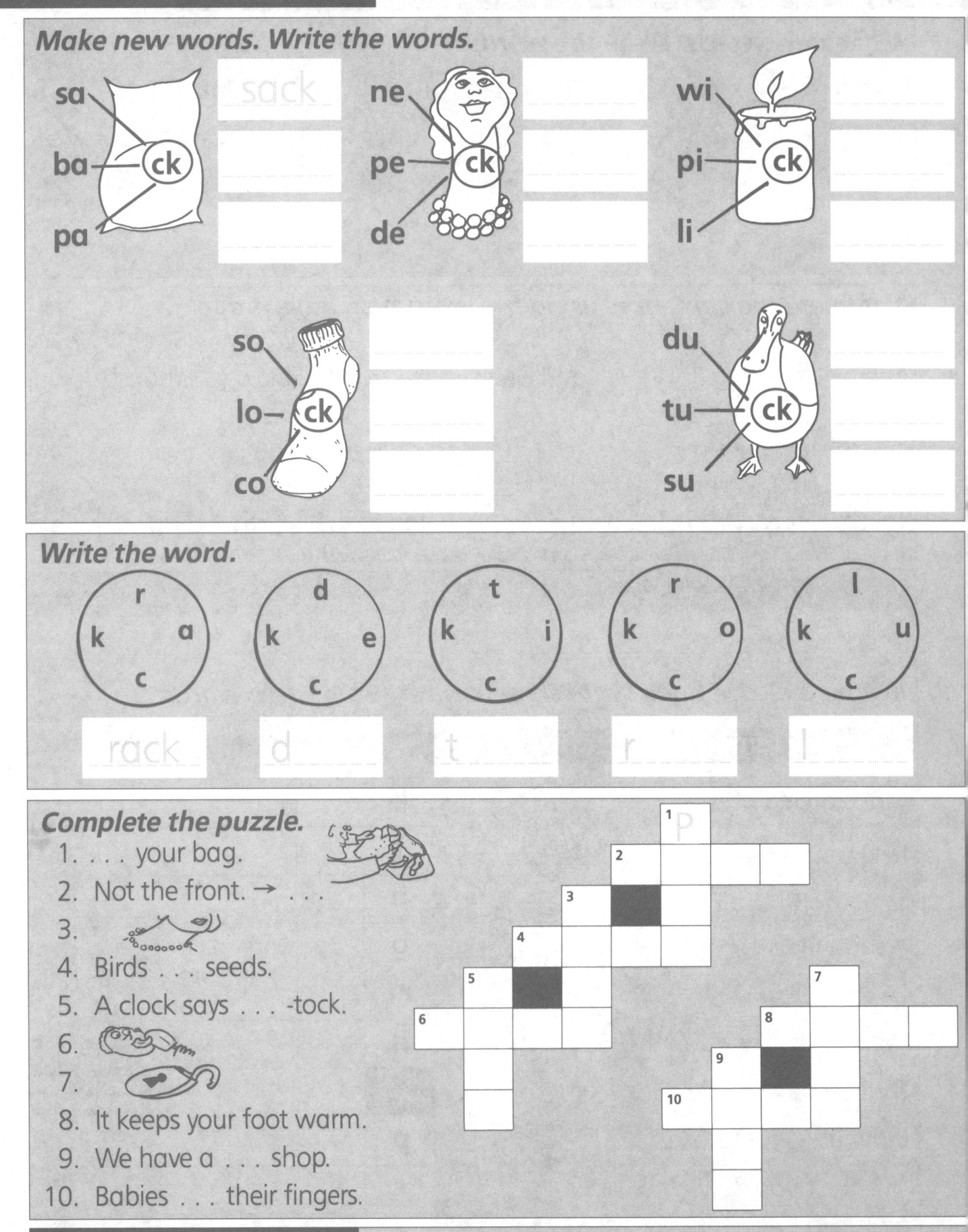

PAGE 20

Make new words. Write the words.

sa · ba · pa — ck → sack

ne · pe · de — ck

wi · pi · li — ck

so · lo · co — ck

du · tu · su — ck

Write the word.

r, k, a, c → rack

d, k, e, c → d___

t, k, i, c → t___

r, k, o, c → r___

l, k, u, c → l___

Complete the puzzle.

1. . . . your bag.
2. Not the front. → . . .
3. (fish image)
4. Birds . . . seeds.
5. A clock says . . . -tock.
6. (mouse image)
7. (lock image)
8. It keeps your foot warm.
9. We have a . . . shop.
10. Babies . . . their fingers.

Write Read Learn Spell

back sack deck neck lick pick lock sock duck luck

In your exercise book write ten sentences using these words.

'–ng' as in 'king'

Make new words. Write the words.

ki		ba		hu	
ri		sa		ru	
wi	ng	ha	ng	su	ng
si		ra		lu	
di		ga		bu	

lo	go	so	do
		ng	

Complete the puzzle.

1. (ring)
2. (king)
3. (rung — ladder)
4. (gong)
5. (gang)
6. (wing)
7. Not short.
8. A loud noise.
9. (sing — choir)
10. Something you sing.
11. The bell . . . .
12. Like a cork.

Write Read Learn Spell

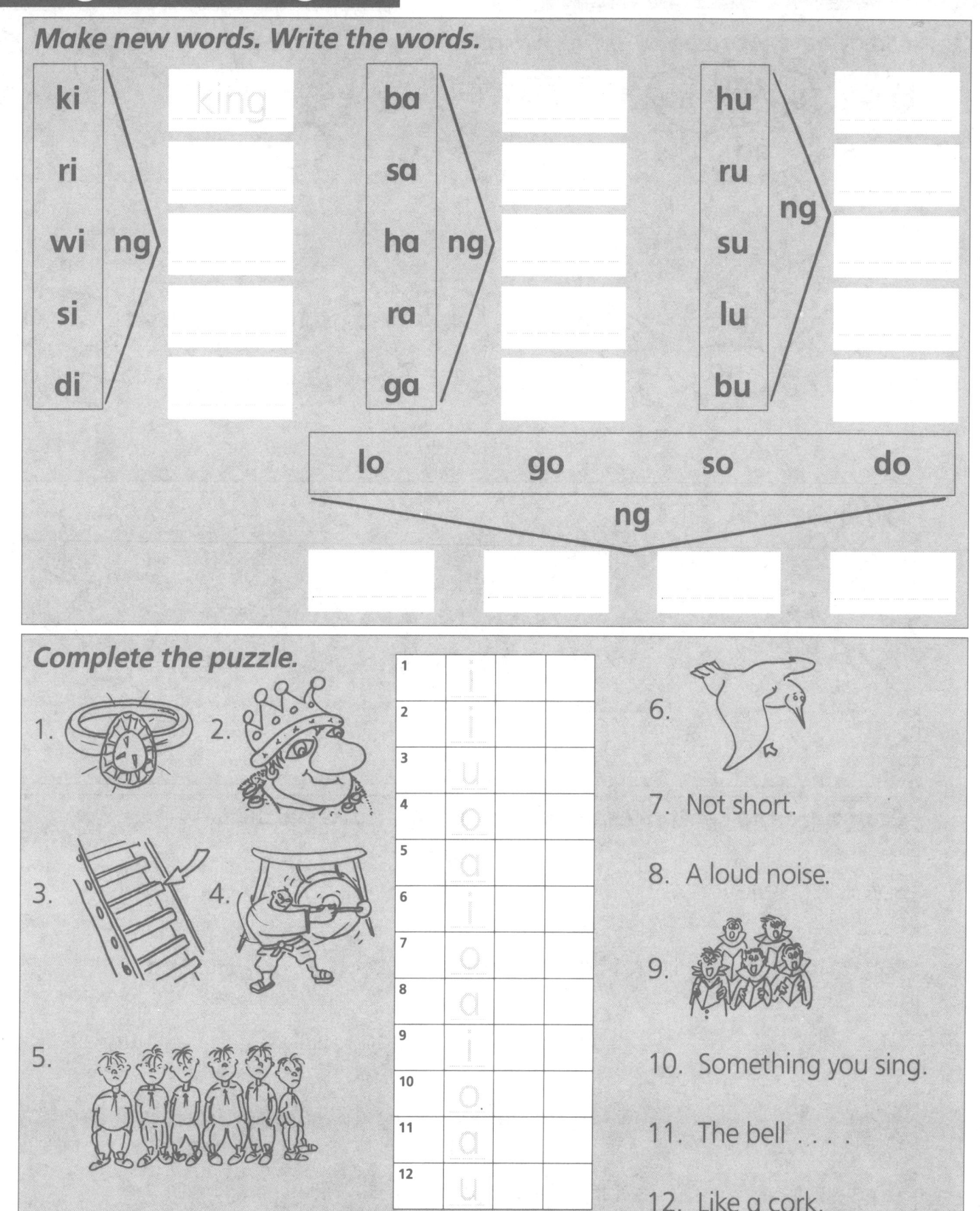

king ring sing wing bang hang long hung sung ding-dong

In your exercise book write ten sentences using these words.

PAGE 21

'–nd' as in 'pond'

PAGE 22

Make new words. Write the words.

ba, la, sa, ha + nd

band

e, be, se, me, le + nd

fu, bo, po + nd

ki, fi, wi, mi + nd

Write the word.

pond

Complete the sentences using words you have made.

Some fish swim in a pond .

I hold my pen in my _____.

I dig in the _____ on the seashore.

We live on _____.

Mum has to _____ my socks.

Dad has to _____ up the clock.

There is a _____ in the road.

I cannot _____ my book.

An elastic _____ holds things together.

This is the _____.

Write Read Learn Spell

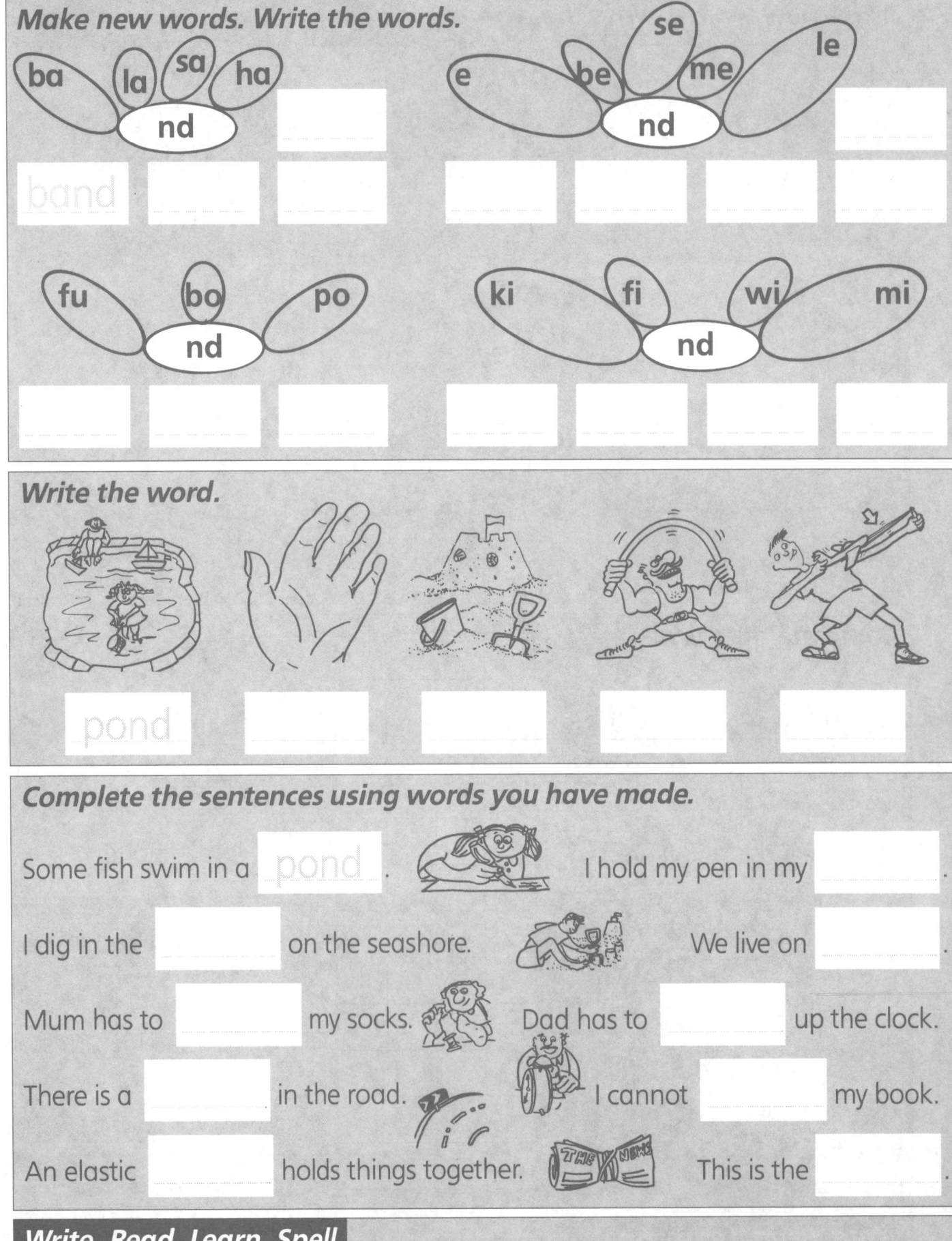

pond hand land sand end bend lend send kind find

In your exercise book write ten sentences using these words.

Can you remember?

PAGE 23

– ck   – ng   – nd   Write the word.

Complete the words in the puzzle.

He rules the land ....
A noise ....
You sing this ....
Not the front – the ....
Part of a ship ....
Not short ....
Castles are made with this on the beach ....
It blows ....
To repair something ....
The clock says . . . -tock ....

k			
			g
s			
			k
d			
			g
		n	
w			
			d
			k

Find six words in the snake. The last letter of each word starts the new word.

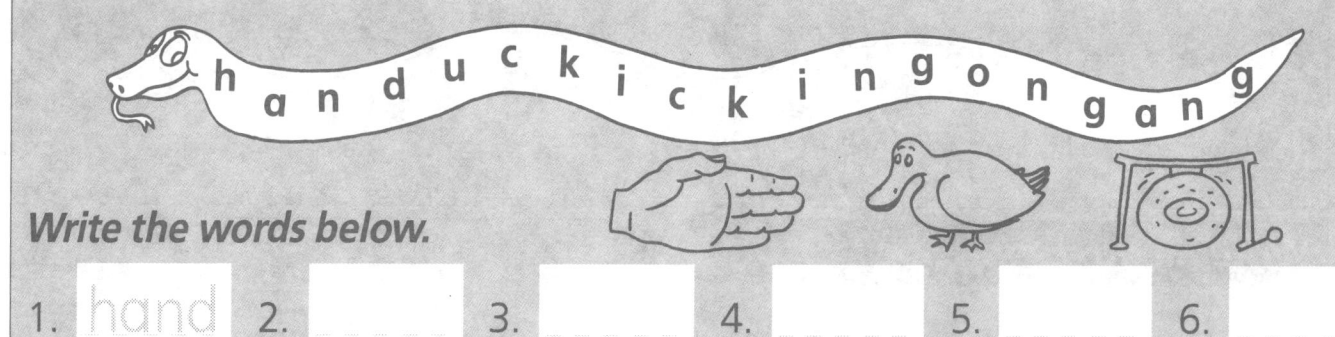

h a n d u c k i c k i n g o n g a n g

Write the words below.

1. hand   2. _____   3. _____   4. _____   5. _____   6. _____

In your exercise book use five of these words in sentences.

Pets

PAGE 24

7. fish
9. bird
3. pony
2. cat
8. hamster
10. snake
6. rabbit
4. mouse
5. kitten
1. dog

Write the names of ten pets you can see in the picture.

1.
2.
3.
4.
5.
6.
7.
8.
9.
10.

Fill in the missing letters. Complete the word.

mo_s_   _b_d   s_a_e

_k_t_en   h_mst_r   _p_n_

Write Read Learn Spell

pony mouse kitten rabbit fish hamster bird snake

In your exercise book write ten sentences using these words.

Seashore

PAGE 25

Labels in picture:
1. sea
2. waves
3. sand
4. bucket
5. spade
6. gulls
7. pool
8. rock
9. crab
10. swim

Write the words from the picture.

1. _____
2. _____
3. _____
4. _____
5. _____
6. _____
7. _____
8. _____
9. _____
10. _____

Complete the sentences by using the words you have written above.

I dig in the _____ with my _____ .

The _____ splash us.

Mum can _____ in the _____ .

I fill my _____ with water.

The _____ fly in the sky.

A _____ walks sideways.

There is a little fish in the _____ .

Find the word. Write it.

w v / s a e — waves
c r / o k — rock
s a / e — sea
c / b r a — crab
n / a d s — sand

Write Read Learn Spell

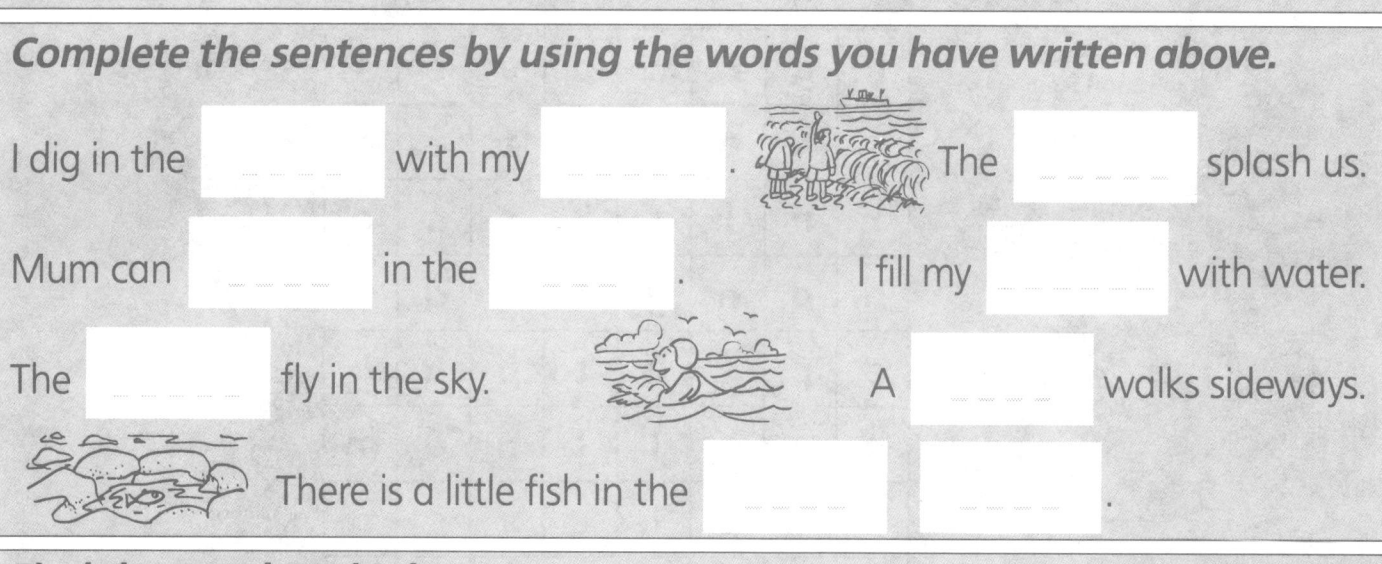

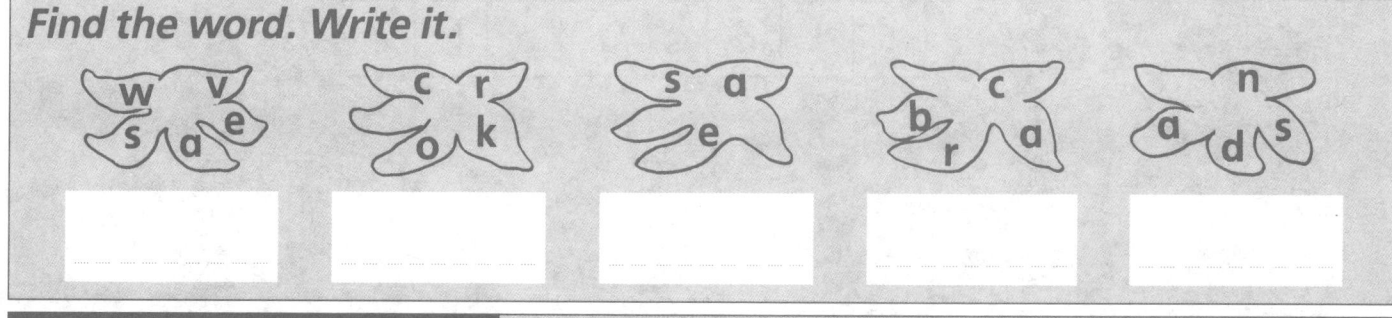

sea waves sand bucket spade gulls pool rock crab swim

In your exercise book write ten sentences using these words.

Can you remember?

PAGE 26

Pets and the seashore. Write the word.

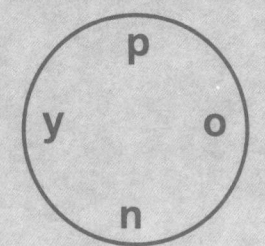

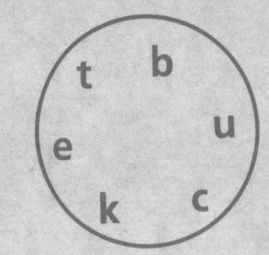

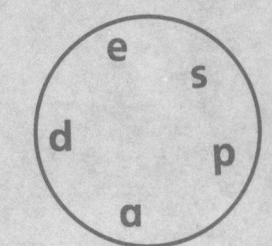

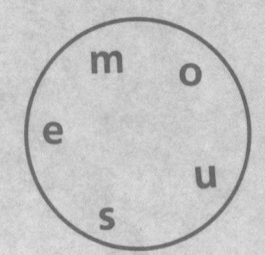

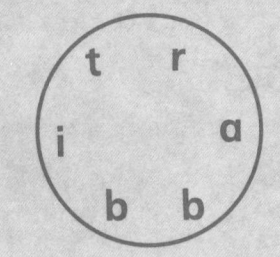

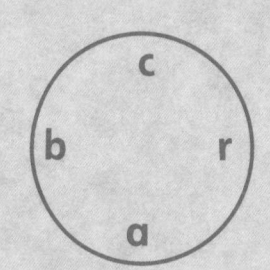

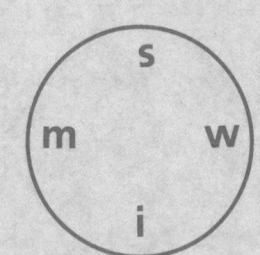

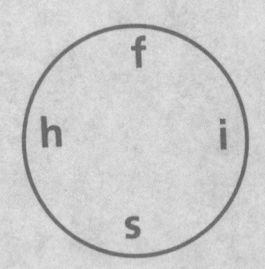

(Letter circles: pony; bucket; spade; mouse)

(Letter circles: rabbit; crab; swim; fish)

Find ten words. Look across or down. Ring each word. Write the word.

b	g	b	w	a	v	e	s
i	h	a	m	s	t	e	r
r	n	i	r	k	s	s	o
d	a	n	g	i	r	a	c
e	p	l	u	t	p	n	k
n	o	a	l	t	o	d	m
o	o	p	l	e	s	e	q
t	l	e	s	n	a	k	e

1.
2.
3.
4.
5.
6.
7.
8.
9.
10.

Birthdays

PAGE 27

1. card
2. present
3. cake
4. candles
5. party
6. jelly
7. game
8. happy
9. boys
10. girls

Write the words from the picture.

Find the word. Write it.

Complete the sentences using the words you have written.

It is Ben's birthday.   He has a _____ from Emma.

His _____ has a badge on it.   He has a big birthday _____.

It has six _____.   The _____ are eating _____.

The _____ are playing a _____.   Everyone is _____.

Write Read Learn Spell

card present cake candles party jelly games happy boys girls

In your exercise book write ten sentences using these words.

Numbers in words (1-10)

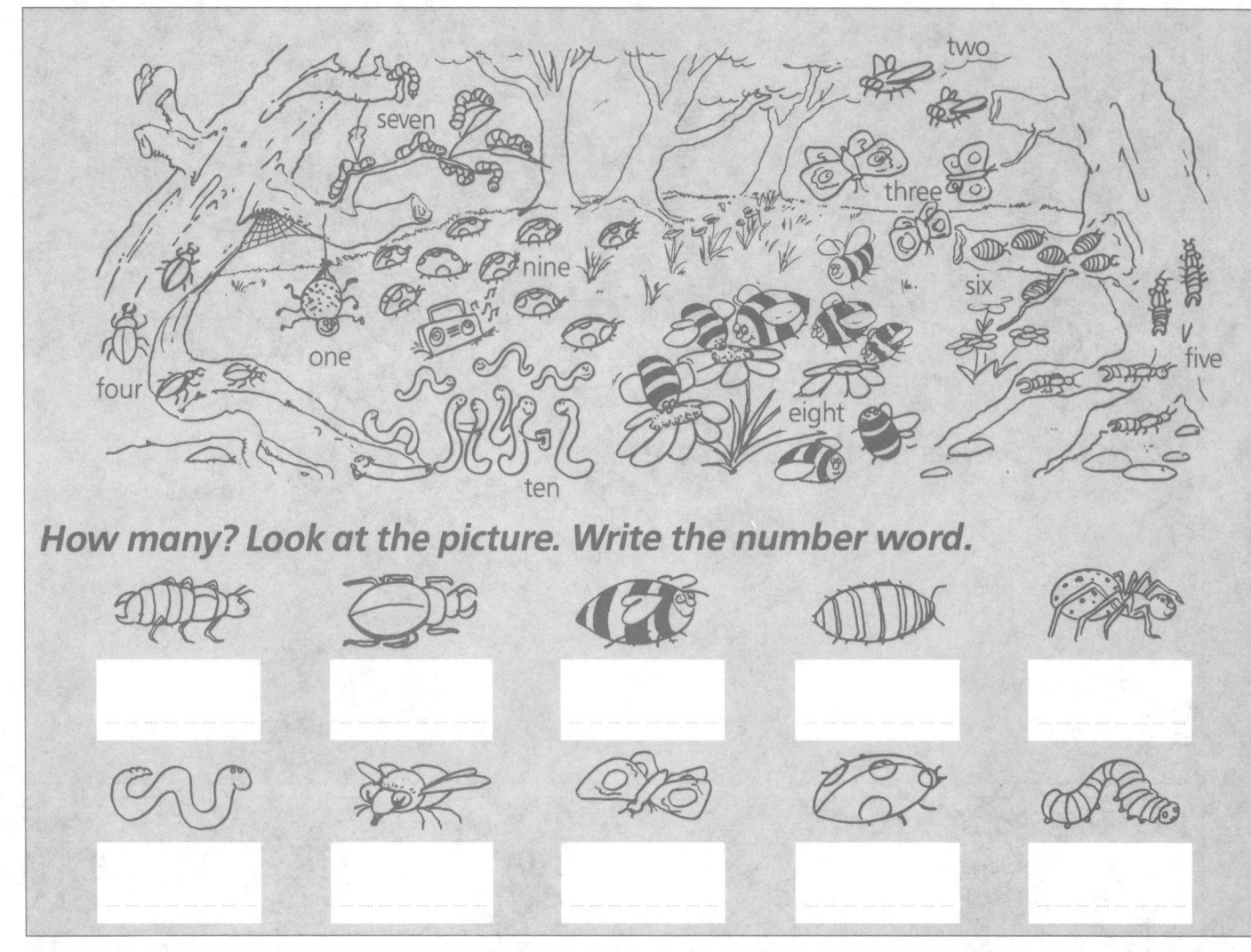

PAGE 28

How many? Look at the picture. Write the number word.

Complete the puzzle.

1. four

Write Read Learn Spell

one two three four five six seven eight nine ten

In your exercise book write ten sentences using these words.

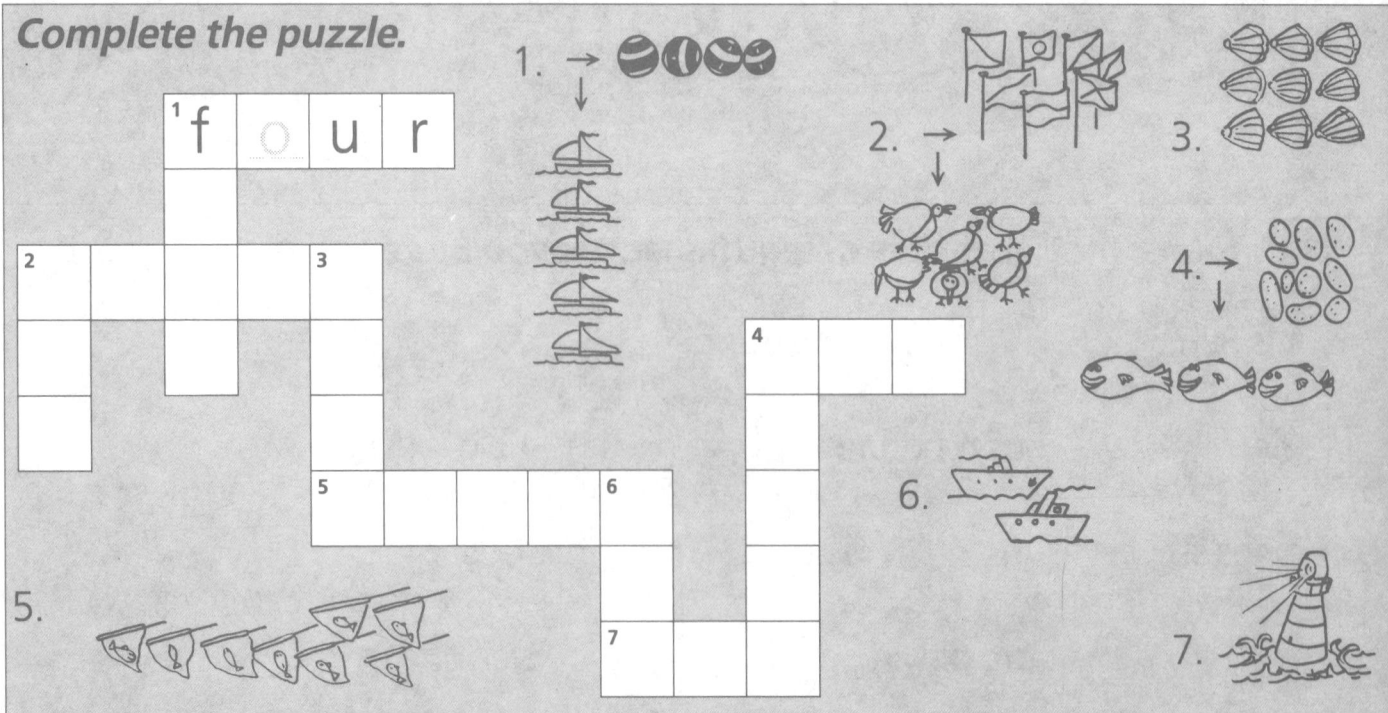

Can you remember?

PAGE 29

Complete the puzzle.

1. Not down.
2. [picture of party]
3. [picture of birthday card]
4. You play . . . at a party.
5. [picture of two people laughing]
6. [picture of present]
7. [picture of children kissing]
8. [picture of sandwiches]
9. A knock . . . the door.
10. Not out.
11. Not she.
12. Not off.
13. [picture of jelly]
14. . . . are going to school.
15. ↓ The flower . . . red.
16. [picture of three boys]
17. Not on.
18. A cup . . . tea.

Early Spellings

Titles available: Books 1-3

Develops spelling skills through
- focus on spelling patterns
- establishing the link between reading & writing
- enjoyable context-driven spelling activities

KEY STAGE 1/2

Other series from Schofield & Sims Ltd:

	Maths & Science	Language & Literacy
Early Learning	**Workbooks:** Nursery Activity Books	**Workbooks:** Early Writing Books, Nursery Activity Books, Nursery Writing Books
Key Stage 1	**Workbooks:** Key Maths, Number Books	**Workbooks:** Basic Skills, First Phonics, Sound Practice **Readers:** Play Words, Read with the Riddlers, Read and Colour **Dictionaries:** My Picture Dictionary, My First Picture Dictionary **Word books:** Picture Words, Early Words, Topic Words **Copymasters:** Reading Comprehension KS 1
Bridging Key Stages 1 & 2	**Workbooks:** Times Tables, Starting Science **Programmes:** Maths Quest **Games:** Master Pieces	**Workbooks:** Early Spellings **Programmes:** Journeys in Reading, Oracy, Study Reading **Dictionaries:** Illustrated Dictionary, Bilingual Dictionaries **Word books:** First Words, Early Words **Copymasters:** Reading Comprehension Bridging Pack **Games:** Master Pieces
Key Stage 2	**Workbooks:** Mental Arithmetic, Times Tables, Homework, Progress Papers – Maths **Practice:** Number Practice, Alpha/Beta, More Practice **Assessment:** Assessment Papers in Maths, Assessment Papers in Science, Practice SATs – Maths	**Workbooks:** Springboard, Spellaway, Key Spellings, Homework, Spelling Practice, Progress Papers – English, Progress Papers – Reasoning **Programmes:** English Skills **Dictionaries:** Keyword Dictionary, Easy Dictionary, Concise Junior Dictionary, Basic Dictionary, Compact Dictionary, Simplified Dictionary, Spelling Dictionary **Word books:** Better Words, In Other Words, Choose Your Words, Use Your Words, Classified Spelling **Assessments:** Assessment Papers in English, Practice SATs – Explorers, Practice SATs – Bicycles **Copymasters:** Reading Comprehension KS 2, English Practice, Big on Books – Guided Activities for KS 2 Literacy Hour

Schofield & Sims Ltd, Huddersfield, England
Tel: 01484 607080 Fax: 01484 606815

WHSmith £1·99

ISBN 0-7217-0667-3